D0974601

Daughter,
this reminder from my heart
expresses all my special
thoughts and feelings for you —
because sometimes I forget to tell you
how very much you mean to me.

— Barbara J. Hall

Blue Mountain Arts®

New and Best-Selling Titles

By Susan Polis Schutz:

To My Daughter with Love on the Important Things in Life

To My Son with Love

By Douglas Pagels:

For You, My Soul Mate

Required Reading for All Teenagers

The Next Chapter of Your Life

You Are One Amazing Lady

By Marci:

Angels Are Everywhere!

Friends Are Forever

10 Simple Things to Remember

To My Daughter

To My Granddaughter

To My Son

You Are My "Once in a Lifetime"

By Wally Amos, with Stu Glauberman:

The Path to Success Is Paved with Positive Thinking

By Minx Boren:

Healing Is a Journey

By Carol Wiseman:

Emerging from the Heartache of Loss

Anthologies:

A Daughter Is Life's Greatest Gift

A Daybook of Positive Thinking

A Son Is Life's Greatest Gift

Dream Big, Stay Positive, and Believe in Yourself

Girlfriends Are the Best Friends of All

God Is Always Watching Over You

God Loves You Just the Way You Are

Hang In There

The Love Between a Mother and Daughter Is Forever

Nothing Fills the Heart with Joy like a Grandson

There Is Nothing Sweeter in Life Than a Granddaughter

There Is So Much to Love About You... Daughter

Think Positive Thoughts Every Day

When I Say I Love You

Words Every Woman Should Remember

There Is So Much to Love About You... Daughter

A Blue Mountain Arts® Collection

Edited by Patricia Wayant

Blue Mountain Press™
Boulder, Colorado

Copyright © 2009 by Blue Mountain Arts, Inc.

All rights reserved. No part of this publication may be reproduced, stored in a retrieval system or transmitted in any form or by any means, electronic, mechanical, photocopying, recording or otherwise, without the written permission of the publisher.

We wish to thank Susan Polis Schutz for permission to reprint the following poems that appear in this publication: "The love of a family...," "When you need someone...," "When you were born...," "Find happiness in nature...," "You are a shining example...," "Let me tell you how...," "My day becomes wonderful...," "Lean against a tree...," "I looked at you today...," and "A daughter is...." Copyright © 1980, 1982, 1983, 1984, 1986, 1991 by Stephen Schutz and Susan Polis Schutz. And for "It is so important...." Copyright © 1979 by Continental Publications. All rights reserved.

Library of Congress Control Number: 2009930507
ISBN: 978-1-59842-871-1 (previously ISBN: 978-1-59842-445-4)

and Blue Mountain Press are registered in U.S. Patent and Trademark Office.
Certain trademarks are used under license.

Acknowledgments appear on page 124.

Printed in China.
First printing of this edition: 2015

This book is printed on recycled paper.

This book is printed on paper that has been specially produced to be acid free (neutral pH) and contains no groundwood or unbleached pulp. It conforms with the requirements of the American National Standards Institute, Inc., so as to ensure that this book will last and be enjoyed by future generations.

Blue Mountain Arts, Inc.
P.O. Box 4549, Boulder, Colorado 80306

Contents

There Is So Much to Love About You... Daughter

I've been so proud of you throughout the years. With exquisite joy and delight, I have watched you grow and marveled at the mysteries and curiosities of each stage unraveling before my eyes. You've made me so happy; your love has kept me solid through my own journey in life.

I look at you now and see such beauty in the woman you are becoming, and I'm so glad that you've stayed close to me. It means so much when you ask for my advice or opinion on things. We have a mutual respect for each other that continues to strengthen.

I love to talk with you about anything... serious or light. And I love that we can laugh together not only as parent and daughter, but as the very best of friends.

I want you to know how I feel about you. You have enriched my life more than you'll ever know, and you have taught me so much about being a parent, a friend... and a person. I love you, and I'm so very proud of you. Please know that no matter where you may be or where you will go, I'll be right there with you... in a special place in your heart.

— Debbie Burton-Peddle

You Are Life's Greatest Gift to Me

Memories come flooding back to me
as I look back over the years.
I want to hold on to you
and at the same time
watch you fly high and free.
You have such spirit
and a character all your own.
You are a doer and an achiever
of what you believe in.
I'm so proud of the dreams you have
and the conviction you have
to make those dreams come true.
Your world is bright, new,
and bursting with possibilities.

It's so easy to remember
your very first steps
and how I held out my hand
for you to hold.
As each year passes
you take more steps,
and some of these will eventually
lead you away from me —
but always remember that my hand
and my heart are forever here for you.
You will always be my daughter,
but I have also discovered in you
a rare and precious friend.
You have been life's greatest gift to me,
and I love you so much.

— Vickie M. Worsham

What Is a Daughter?

A daughter is one of the greatest blessings
one could ever have
She begins her life loving and trusting you
automatically

For many years, you are the center of her life
Together you experience the delights of
the new things she learns and does

You enter into her play and are once again young
And even though it's harder to enter into her
world as she becomes a teen...

You are there, understanding her dilemmas and
her fears
And wishing with all your heart that she didn't
have to go through them

A daughter's smile is a precious sight that
you treasure each time you see it
And the sound of her laughter always brings
joy to your heart

Her successes mean more to you than your own
And her happiness is your happiness

Her heartaches and disappointments
become yours, too
Because when she isn't okay, you can't
be okay either...

Daughters aren't perfect
but you, Daughter, come close
You have given me more happiness than you know

I am thankful for your kindness and
thoughtfulness
And I am proud of who you are
and how you live your life

Words can't express how much you mean
to me or how much I love you
The love goes too deep, and the gratitude
and pride I feel are boundless

Thank you for blessing my life
in so many ways

— Barbara Cage

A daughter is...
a star glimmering in the sky
a wonder, a sweetness
a perception, a delight...
everything beautiful
A daughter is
love

— Susan Polis Schutz

When a Daughter Is Born...

In that moment when you took your first breath, Daughter, I realized that I was about to take my first breath, too. Everything I needed that day was wrapped in a tiny blanket and placed next to my heart — where you have grown and blossomed into a beautiful and amazing woman.

— Debra Cavatio

When you were born
I held you in my arms
and just kept smiling at you
You always smiled back
your big eyes wide open
full of love
You were such a
beautiful
good
sweet baby
Now as I watch you grow up
and become your own person
I look at you
your laughter
your happiness
your simplicity
your beauty
And I know that you will
be able to enjoy a life
of sensitivity
goodness
accomplishment
and love

— Susan Polis Schutz

This Is What I See When I Look at You...

I see a gorgeous butterfly
emerging from her cocoon —
someone who is growing and changing,
becoming more beautiful each
and every day.
I see a young woman who is ready
to take on the world and
whatever it throws her way.
Where there was once a child,
there is now an adult —
someone who stands up for herself
and for those she loves,
someone who offers a helpful hand,
a shoulder to cry on,
and a kind word when she knows
someone is down.
I see an angel here on earth.

— Shannon Koehler

Whenever I am in your presence, I know I am looking at the smiling face of one of the most wonderful people I will ever have the privilege of knowing.

Whenever I am reminded of you, I find so many hopes and memories in my heart. They're my favorite treasures, and nothing warms my heart like they do.

Whenever I think of you, I think of how precious you've always been and how close I hope we'll always be.

If I could be given any gift imaginable, one that would make me happy beyond words, make me feel truly blessed, and make my days just shine...

The gift I'd choose would be you... each and every time.

— Terry Bairnson

Did You Know That I Loved You Long Before You Were Born?

When I first held you in my arms,
one of my dreams came true.
I remember staring at your perfect little features
and feeling thrilled at each new sound
and expression.
A fierce need to protect you came over me then,
and it has never gone away.
When you were a child,
I was able to hold you close through illness
and heartache,
and my presence and guidance seemed to
assure you of a certain level of safety.

But little by little, I have had to let you go
and allow you to make your own way.
So often I wanted to call you back
and have you stay in the protective circle
of my arms.
I never wanted you to have to face injury
or heartache,
yet I knew that you had to in order to grow.
Now you are making your own decisions.
Just remember that no matter what, I love you.
I could never stop loving you.
You are the hugs and smiles from my past,
the hopes and dreams of my future.
Take care, my daughter,
and know that you are never alone.
We are connected by the strongest bond there is:
the love between parent and child.

— Barbara Cage

If I Could Teach You Only One Thing in Life It Would Be to Love...

To respect others so that you may
find respect in yourself
To learn the value of giving, so if
ever there comes a time in your
life when someone is really in need,
you will give
To act in a manner that you would
wish to be treated
To be proud of yourself
To laugh and smile as much as you
can in order to help bring joy
back into this world
To have faith in others
To be understanding
To stand tall in this world and
to learn to depend on yourself

To only take from this earth those
things you really need, so there
will be enough for others
To not depend on money or
material things for your happiness
To learn to appreciate the people who
love you and the simple beauty
that God gave you
To find peace and security within
yourself

To you, my child, I hope I have
taught all of these things,
for they are love.

— Donna Dargis

Always Have at Least One True Friend

Some of the luckiest people in the world are those who have a wonderful friend to share life with... A friend who cares and who shares the gifts of smiles and closeness and companionship. Someone with whom you have so much in common. Somebody who's a precious part of the best memories you'll ever make. A special friend. A true friend. One to confide in, one who never lets you down, and one who always understands. A friend who has a heart that is so big and a soul that is so beautiful, and everything about them inspires everything that is good about you.

— Douglas Pagels

The heart needs friendship to make us feel that we belong in life. We need special people who accept us just as we are, who make us laugh when we need to, who cry with us when we're sad, who celebrate with us when we're up, and who are there for us when we're down.

We need people in our lives with whom we can share our everyday thoughts, form a bond, and grow old — people who won't desert us and on whom we can really depend.

— Donna Fargo

Remember Who You Are

Don't ever lose sight of the gift that is you. When life seems to knock you down, get back up and get back in the game.

Remember what you're made of. Remember what's flowing in your veins. Remember what you were given, and remember what you went out and created on your own. Like any great masterpiece, you're not done yet. Inside you is the best of everyone who has come before you — and the best of everyone yet to be. You can forget some of what life hands you, but never, ever forget who you are.

— Rachel Snyder

Let me tell you how others see you
(including me)
We see a pretty, loving, caring
sensitive, intelligent person
who has all the qualities necessary
to become a very successful
and beautiful woman
yet sometimes it seems that you do not have
a high enough opinion of yourself
You compare yourself unfavorably to others
Please don't be so hard on yourself
Look in the mirror and see the
extraordinary person that you already are
and believe how much
you are loved and appreciated

— Susan Polis Schutz

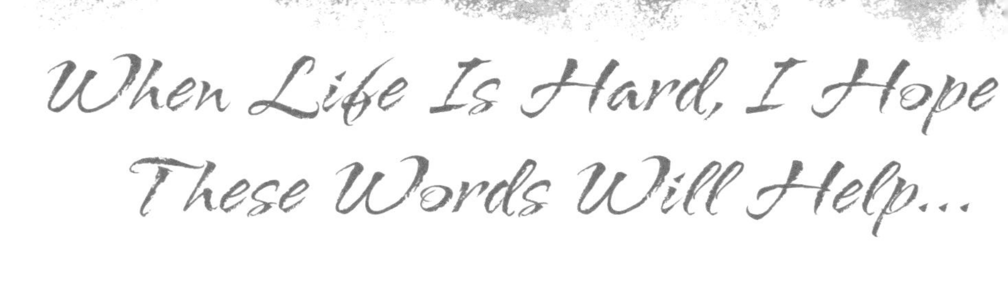

When Life Is Hard, I Hope These Words Will Help...

Your life can be
 what you want it to be...
You'll make it through
 whatever comes along.

Within you are so many answers.
 Understand, have courage,
 be strong.

— Douglas Pagels

You have the courage and strength to overcome many obstacles. No matter how many times you fall, you can get up again.

You have a big heart. You make everyone around you feel loved. You touch so many lives without even knowing it.

You have been blessed with not only outer beauty but inner beauty. This is the kind of beauty that is everlasting. Time can never take that away from you.

— Mary Adisano

The Absolutely True Story of One Amazing Girl... You!

Once there was a girl, and she was unique and talented and interesting and amazing and unforgettable... and real. She knew, deep down, that if she tried something and it didn't go as she had hoped or wanted or dreamed or planned, she could just try something different — or try the same thing again but approach it in a new or different way — and one day her greatest hopes and dreams could actually come true.

And so her life was full of all these amazing and unforgettable moments, events, and circumstances: incredible wins, of course, but also equally incredible — and worth it — losses. No matter what happened, she learned from everything around her and everything she went through. Yes, she fell sometimes (like everybody else does), but she got up and moved forward by always being true to herself. She hoped that maybe one day she could even make a path for others to follow... until they each could make their own paths, too.

You see, it's not that she was never frightened or sad or even knew when she woke up each day what to do (no one does). It was simply that she believed in herself and always shined on like a star. Just like you.

— Ashley Rice

You have powers you never dreamed of. You can do things you never thought you could do. There are no limitations in what you can do except the limitations in your own mind as to what you cannot do. Don't think you cannot. Think you can.

— Darwin P. Kingsley

It is so important
to choose your own
lifestyle
and not let others
choose it for you

— Susan Polis Schutz

Do not follow where
the path may lead.
Go, instead, where
there is no path
and leave a trail.

— Anonymous

I Have So Many Dreams for You, Daughter

I dream for your happiness. I want you to be happy with who you are and all that your life involves. I dream for you to always know love, for it is what keeps us in touch with what is real and true. I dream for you to live in peace. I want your life to be balanced.

I dream for you to succeed. I want you to achieve your goals and ambitions and to place your priorities carefully. I dream for you to always have good health and harmonious physical, emotional, and spiritual well-being. I dream for you to have a supportive and caring family that loves you beyond measure.

I dream for you to have a solid and secure future. I want good things to come your way and for you to never be in need. I dream for you to have laughter in your life; it is life's natural source for healing.

I dream for you to remain true to yourself. Never lose sight of the wonderful child you once were and the wonderful woman you are today. Remain faithful to your identity, and never let external distractions sway you. Listen to what your heart tells you.

I dream for you to have strength. Life will be good, but there will be tests. I wish for you to build character with life's lessons. Keep your chin up and remain proud.

I dream for you to stay close to me no matter how far away you may be, because nothing and no one will ever change the way I feel about you.

— Debbie Burton-Peddle

Daughter, you have so much to offer,
so much to give, and so much you
deserve to receive in return.
Don't ever doubt that.
Know yourself and all your fine
qualities.
Rejoice in all your marvelous strengths
of mind and body.
Be glad for the virtues that are yours,
and pat yourself on the back for all
your many admirable achievements.

— Janet A. Sullivan

Like a rainbow, you bring
color to ordinary places.

Like a sunset,
you add brilliance.

Like a river,
you know the way.

With the patience of the
forests, you wait for
your dreams to grow.

And like the most special
flower in the garden...

You grow stronger
and more beautiful
every day.

— Ashley Rice

A Daughter Is Never-Ending Love

A daughter is a little piece
    of yourself
looking back at you.
She is another chance for you
    to realize the dreams
        of your past.
She is a precious gift
    and adventures without end.

A daughter is your best creation.
She's a best friend
    and a fashion adviser.
Only she knows why
    you love purple
        and hate turnips.

A daughter is never-ending love,
given and received,
and learning to love yourself.
Of all the things that
happen in life,
a daughter is the best.

— Brenda A. Morris

I Am Continually Cheering for Your Happiness

My day becomes wonderful
when I see your
pretty face smiling so sweetly
There is such warmth and intelligence
radiating from you
It seems that every day
you grow smarter and more beautiful
and every day
I am more proud of you

As you go through different stages of life
you should be aware that there will be many times
when you will feel scared and confused
but with your strength and values
you will always end up wiser
and you will have grown from your experiences
understanding more about people and life
I have already gone through
these stages
So if you need advice or someone to talk to
to make sense out of it all
I hope that you will talk to me
as I am continually cheering for your happiness
my sweet daughter

— Susan Polis Schutz

Don't Let Anything Steal Your Joy

Choose to be well in every way. Choose to be happy no matter what. Decide that each day will be good just because you're alive.

You have power over your thoughts and feelings. Don't let your circumstances dictate how you feel. Don't let your thoughts and feelings color your situation blue or desperate.

Even if you don't have everything you want, even if you're in pain or in need, you can choose to be joyful no matter what you're experiencing. You are more than your body, your physical presence, and your material possessions. You are spirit. You have your mind, heart, and soul, and there is always something to be thankful for.

Decide that life is good and you are special.
Decide to enjoy today. Decide that you will
live life to the fullest now, no matter what.
Trust that you will change what needs
changing, but also decide that you're not
going to put off enjoying life just because
you don't have everything you want now.
Steadfastly refuse to let anything steal your
joy. Choose to be happy... and you will be!

— Donna Fargo

If My Heart Could Speak to You...

Sometimes I forget that you
can't see into my heart
or know what I'm feeling when
I think of you.
This is for the times when
I don't tell you how wonderful you are
or how much I love you
and appreciate your presence in my life.
This reminder from my heart
expresses all my special
thoughts and feelings for you —
because sometimes I forget to tell you
how very much you mean to me.

— Barbara J. Hall

Even
if a day
should go by
when I don't say
"I love you..."

May never a
moment go by
without your
knowing I do

— Daniel Haughian

For All the Times Past and All the Times to Come

For all the times
Our days were relentless
And things seemed so rushed;

For all the times
You grew up a little quicker
Because I couldn't always be there;

For all the times
You heard me angry and frustrated
Or saw me impatient;

For all the times
I thought I was listening
And realized later I hadn't heard you.

I have cried inside again and again
Because maybe what you didn't see were...

All the times
I laughed and boasted about you,
Your ingenuity, your brilliance;

All the times
I sat with a lump in my throat,
Choking back tears of pride
As I watched you perform;

All the times
I noticed how fast you were growing
And changing into a magnificent,
Separate person;

All the times
I marveled at how perfect you were
As I watched you sleep.

For all the times past
And all the times to come,
No one will ever be in my heart
The way you are.

— Laurie Winkelmann

I Am Always Here for You, Daughter

If you ever wonder if anyone cares, know that the love I have for you transcends time and bridges any distance imaginable. Remember: If you ever need me, I will *always* be there... Nothing will ever be as strong as my love and my thankfulness... for you.

— Laurel Atherton

When you need someone
to talk to
I hope you will
talk to me
When you need someone
to laugh with
I hope you will
laugh with me
When you need someone
to advise you
I hope you will
turn to me
When you need someone
to help you
I hope you will
let me help you
I cherish and love
everything about you —
my beautiful daughter
And I will always support you
as a parent, as a person
and as a friend

— Susan Polis Schutz

I'll Always Care

In your happiest and most exciting moments, my
heart will celebrate and smile beside you.
In your lowest lows, my love will be there to keep you
warm, to give you strength, and to remind you
that your sunshine is sure to come again.
In your moments of accomplishment, I will be filled
so full of pride that I may have a hard time
keeping the feeling inside of me.
In your moments of disappointment, I will be a
shoulder to cry on and a hand to hold and a love
that will gently enfold you until everything's okay.
In your gray days, I will help you search, one by one,
for the colors of the rainbow.
In your bright and shining hours, I will be smiling,
too, right along beside you.

In your life, I wish I could give you a very
special gift. It would be this:
When you look in the mirror in the days
ahead, may you smile a hundred times
more than you frown at what you see.
Smile because you know that a loving,
capable, sensible, strong, precious person
is reflected there.

And when you look at me, may you remember
how very much I love you... and how much
I'll always care.

— Laurel Atherton

If I Could Give You Anything It Would Be...

Love — to shine like blue skies above you wherever you go, so you always know you're in the hearts of so many people.

Light — to see the end of the tunnel when you're struggling with troubles, so you always know you have the inner power to survive and triumph.

Lullabies — to fill your mind with highlights of your childhood, so you focus on the good times and great people who nurtured your growth, smiled on your potential, and walked beside you on all the paths toward your dreams.

Laughter — to keep you healthy in mind and body; to give you the ability to tell great jokes, act silly, and exercise your giggle; to remind you that life is too short to be taken so seriously.

A ladder — tall enough for you to climb, so you can reach for your stars.

A lifeline — to anchor you, support you, and keep you going forward in a positive way when you're faced with a crisis, so you always know you are a survivor.

Lots of good luck — to help you fulfill all your wishes, so you always know your possibilities are unlimited... and success is your destiny.

— Jacqueline Schiff

I Have So Many Wishes for You

I wish for you to always see the goodness
in this world,
to do your part in helping those
less fortunate,
to walk hand in hand with those
of less talent,
to follow those with more knowledge,
to be an equal with those who are different.

I wish for you to find your special purpose
in this world so full of choices
and to help lead those who stray.
I wish for you to become your own individual —
to set yourself apart from those who are
the same.
I wish for you the self-confidence to say no
when it is necessary
and the strength to stand alone.

I wish for you the approval of yourself
to love and respect everything that
you are and will become.
I wish for you to reap the fruits
of your talents,
to walk with pride down the road of life,
to be humble in your successes,
and to share in the praises and joy of others.

Most of all, I wish for you to be happy.
For when you are happy,
you have the key that will open all
of the world's doors to you.
Whatever you decide, whoever you become,
my love for you is unconditional;
my arms and heart are always open to you.
My wishes for you are that you will someday
know the joys that only a daughter can bring
and that all your wishes come true.

— Jackie Olson

You Have Always Been a Joy to Me

You have touched my life
with a magic all your own.
There were times when you struggled with me,
longing for your own independence
and searching for your own place in the world.
I tried to hold you close,
knowing all the time in my heart that
it was a part of growing up for you
    and for me,
a part of life we would endure
and that eventually would make us closer
    than ever before.

You are more than a dream come true
for me —
you are a part of my life that will carry on.
And as I watch you changing,
I see a special happiness in all that you do.
With my heart full of memories,
I want you to know that the love we share
has made being a parent
the greatest feeling
I have ever known.

— Deanna Beisser

My Love for You Has a Lifetime Guarantee

You are the sparkle in my eyes
and the pride in my heart.
You are the courage that gives me strength
and the love that gives me life.
You are my inspiration
and the best gift I ever received.

No matter where life's path takes you
or the difficulties you may encounter,
know that I'm with you in spirit.
My love has a lifetime guarantee.
If ever you're in trouble
    or just need a friend,
I'm no further away than a phone call.

— Lois Carruthers

What I Want to Be to You

A place you can come to for comfort.
Eyes you can look at and trust.
A hand you can reach out and clasp.
A heart that understands and doesn't judge.

Someone you can lean on and learn from.
A source of wisdom and loving advice.
A million memories in the making.
A precious companion on the path of life.

A door that is always open.
A caring, gentle hug.
A time that is devoted to family alone.
A lasting reflection of love.

— Douglas Pagels

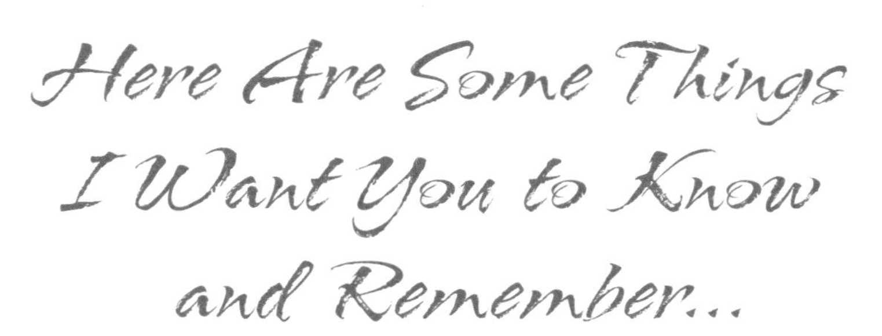

Here Are Some Things I Want You to Know and Remember...

It is with the greatest joy that I am your guardian,
protector, and nurturer,
and I will always strive to fulfill these roles
with honor, trust, and respect for your
thoughts, feelings, and individuality.
What matters most in life are the people you love,
and, for always, you will be one of the people
in my life whom I love the most.

You are the essence of joy and the
true meaning of life.
You are the part of me that I'm most
proud of because you're you.
You are a rare and treasured gift.
You are a dream with all its hope
and promise.
You are love, endless and pure.
You are my beautiful daughter.
Please know and remember this
always.

— Linda Sackett-Morrison

The Best Feeling in the World Is Family

From family we draw love,
friendship, moral support,
and the fulfillment of every
special need within our hearts.
In a family, we are connected to
an ever-present source
of sunny moments, smiles and laughter,
understanding and encouragement,
and hugs that help us grow
in confidence all along life's path.
Wherever we are,
whatever we're doing,
whenever we really need to feel
especially loved, befriended, supported,
and cared for in the greatest way,
our hearts can turn to family
and find the very best
always waiting for us.

— Barbara J. Hall

The love
of a family
is so
uplifting

The warmth
of a family
is so
comforting

The support
of a family
is so
reassuring

The attitude
of a family
toward
each other
molds one's
attitude forever
toward the
world

— Susan Polis Schutz

Fathers and Daughters

Certain it is that there is no kind of affection so purely angelic as that of a father to a daughter. In love to our wives there is desire; to our sons there is ambition; but in that to our daughters there is something which there are no words to express.

— Joseph Addison

When a father looks upon a daughter he bears the love that he bore her mother echoed down through the years.

— Thomas Moore

Remember, dearest little daughter, that you are your papa's only little girl and that his first thought is always and ought to be about you. I never go to sleep without asking all good angels, and especially one, to be near you. You grow dearer and dearer to me the farther I go away from you.

— James Russell Lowell

The lucky man has a daughter as his first child.

— Spanish Proverb

The Story of a Dad and His Daughter

A baby girl is born. Simultaneously, from amid the ranks of ordinary men, there emerges a mightily courageous, gallant man — who is quaking in his shoes.

As they grow together, the girl comes to know that her dad is no ordinary man. He can hear the sound of the sun pushing the clouds out of her world, and he helps her to hear it, too. He can taste the worst cookies that she will make and then eat three or four more from the same batch. He can touch the stars and pull them a little closer to her. He can see the fire of youthful puppy love burning in her heart.

No, this is no ordinary man. He has a body to shield his daughter from strangers, big dogs, and noisy things; a broad expanse of chest to nestle against; and an arm to pillow her head while watching television. He has two strong arms to hold her up to touch the sky, to see inside a bird's nest, or to fly like an airplane.

In her teenage years, he teaches her to respect herself and others. He is always proud of her for trying new things; she doesn't always have to win. He is a wealth of truth in the midst of peer-group untruths, an impatient driving instructor, and a light in the window at twelve o'clock on a Friday night.

In her adulthood, he could choose to slow down a bit, but he won't. He will still utilize his many resources to teach his daughter well, and somehow his mere presence will continue to trigger the potential in her.

He is the firm cornerstone of the family who gives her values to believe in, a heritage she feels worthy of, and an urgency for living her life completely. He is a man who will do anything for his daughter.

— Elaine C. Frantz

Mothers and Daughters

The love between a mother and daughter
is a bond of the strongest kind.
It is a love of the present,
interwoven with memories of the past
and dreams of the future.
It is strengthened by overcoming obstacles
and facing fears and challenges together.
It is having pride in each other
and knowing that your love
can withstand anything.
It is sacrifice and tears,
laughter and hugs.

It is understanding, patience,
and believing in each other.
It is wanting only the best for each other
and wanting to help anytime
there is a need.
It is respect, a hug,
and unexpected kindness.
It is making time to be together
and knowing just what to do and say.
It is an unconditional,
forever kind of love.

— Barbara Cage

What Being Your Mother Means to Me

Being your mother means that I have had the opportunity to experience loving someone more than I love myself. I have learned what it's like to experience joy and pain through someone else's life.

It has brought me pride and joy; your accomplishments touch me and thrill me like no one else's can. It has brought me a few tears and heartaches at times, but it has taught me hope and patience. It has shown me the depth, strength, and power of love.

It hasn't always been easy, and I'm sure I've said and done things that have hurt or confused you. But no one has ever made me as satisfied as you do just by being happy. No one has made me as proud as you do just by living up to your responsibilities.

No one's smile has ever warmed my heart like yours does; no one's laughter fills me with delight as quickly as yours can. No one's hugs feel as sweet, and no one's dreams mean as much to me as yours do.

No other memories of bad times have miraculously turned into important lessons or humorous stories; the good times have become precious treasures to relive again and again.

You are a part of me, and no matter what happened in the past or what the future holds, you are someone I will always accept, forgive, appreciate, adore, and love unconditionally.

Being your mother means that I've been given one of life's greatest gifts: you.

— Barbara Cage

When a Daughter Becomes a Friend

Through the years, I watched you grow, change, and constantly question everything. When you were little, there was an overwhelming feeling inside me that wanted to hold you close and keep you safe and warm all your life. Yet as the years passed, I realized that I couldn't do that. You have always been a child full of wonder, and to keep you so close to me would have deprived you of experiencing life's wonders.

Now, after years of letting you go your own way and watching you become a beautiful young lady, our roles have changed. You are still my daughter, and I am still your parent...

...but most precious of all is the fact that we have become good friends, and we have a friendship that will stand the test of time.

I'll always cherish the wonder and joy of watching you grow into a beautiful young lady. I'll always be proud to say, "This is my daughter." But most of all, I'm proud to say that you are my best friend.

— Vicky Lafleur

Growing and Learning Together

Throughout the years, just watching my daughter grow from childhood to adulthood has brought me more pleasure than anyone could know. From her I have learned that life's most precious gift is the family around us.

— Linda E. Knight

What I treasure most is the love that has grown between us. Maybe it's because we have grown in our own ways and in our own times to be more receptive to what is really important in our lives.

— Elizabeth Hornsey Reeves

Through your eyes, Daughter, I learned how to love, smile from within, and live a happy life. Your eyes told me every day that even if no one else in this world ever needed me, you always would. You could look into my eyes and assure me that we would grow together and become best friends, and that's just what we did. I learned how to appreciate the blessing of a child and the beauty of motherhood. You are the reason I have memories to keep forever and a future to look forward to. You are my heart and soul.

— Debra Cavatio

I Want to Thank You...

For all the smiles and good times,
For the opportunity to share
your life's experiences,
For the trust you've always placed in me,
And for being the best daughter
anyone could ever ask for.

— Anna Marie Edwards

You truly are a treasure to me,
and I will cherish you all my life.
I will brag about you and show you off
every time I get the chance.
And though I don't know how it's possible,
you become more dear to me
with every year that passes by.

— Cheryl Barker

Great Things About Daughters...

- ♡ They keep you young at heart.
- ♡ They continually impress you with their knowledge and capabilities.
- ♡ They tell you about new trends, new movies, and new musical groups.
- ♡ They give excellent fashion advice.
- ♡ They stand up for what they believe in.
- ♡ They always want to help.

Daughters Are...

- ♡ Appreciated.
- ♡ Adored.
- ♡ Looked on with pride.
- ♡ Rays of sunshine.
- ♡ Beautiful inside and out.
- ♡ Irreplaceable members of the family.
- ♡ A part of so many treasured memories.

My Hope for You, Daughter

I can't give you the world,
filled with all its riches.
I can't promise you a life free from
sickness, pain, and disappointment,
for that is a gift not mine to give.
I cannot guarantee that you
will never feel your heart break.
My only hope for you is that
you fulfill the dreams deep within you.

I wish for you to know yourself
and be faithful to yourself.
For if you do,
you will be able to fully love others.
Be free to choose your course in life
without fearing a wrong decision.
Reflect on what you have been taught,
and take time to listen to your heart.
Never lose the ability to feel with open arms
all the passion and joy that life holds for you.
Give all you have
without looking for something in return.
Reach out for that which you can attain
and not for that which is impossible.
My hope for you, my daughter,
is that you will be all you can be,
for only then will you awaken
to the person you want to be.

— Joan Benicken

Ten Golden Rules to Help You Have a Better Life

1. Live your life with purpose; don't just do "whatever," or "whatever" might just be what you get.

2. Develop a compassionate spirit and a loving heart; you will feel better about yourself, and others will feel better about you.

3. Be honest and guard your integrity no matter what the rest of the world is doing; they're not the ones who have to live with you — you are.

4. Believe in yourself and always do what's right; a clear conscience will keep you on the right path.

5. Be as good as your word and don't make promises you're not going to keep.

6. Be fair to others, especially those less fortunate; there may come a time you have to walk in their shoes.

7. Keep a positive attitude and speak encouraging words; you'll hear them rise up in you when you need them, and others will remember them when they need lifting up.

8. Don't take your natural talents for granted; use them to nourish your soul and to touch lives, and they will be multiplied.

9. When you feel discouraged or unlucky, remember the times you've been fortunate, and that knowledge will help balance out your fears.

10. Remember that what you do today will show up tomorrow, so when you make important decisions, think about tomorrow today.

— Donna Fargo

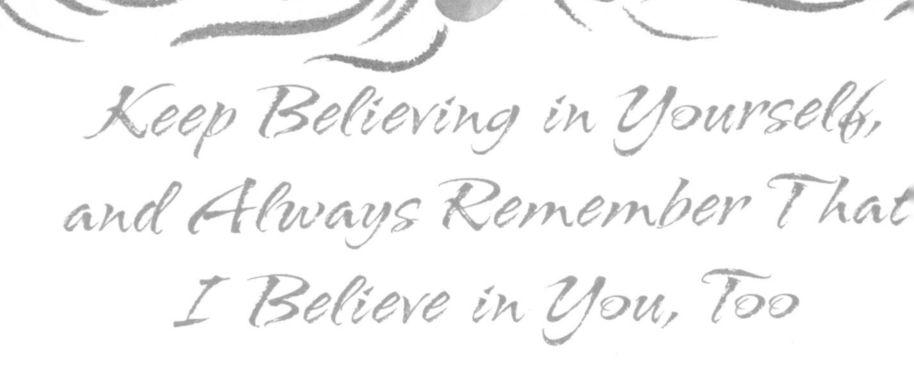

Keep Believing in Yourself, and Always Remember That I Believe in You, Too

Every goal that has ever
been reached began with just
one step — and the belief
that it could be attained.

Dreams really can come true,
but they are most often the result
of hard work, determination,
and persistence.

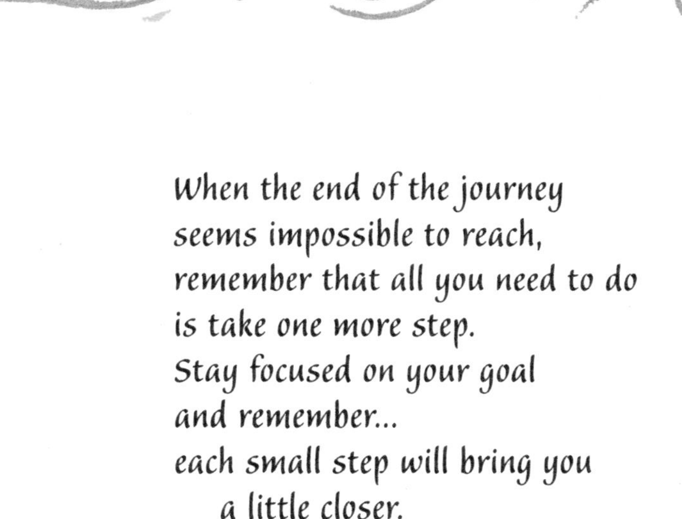

When the end of the journey
seems impossible to reach,
remember that all you need to do
is take one more step.
Stay focused on your goal
and remember...
each small step will bring you
a little closer.
Look deep inside your heart
and you will find strength
you never knew you had.

Believe in yourself —
and remember that
I believe in you, too.

— Jason Blume

Be True to the Light Inside You

Never let anyone change your mind about what you feel you can achieve.

Be true to the light that is deep within you. Hold on to your faith, hope, and joy for life. Keep good thoughts in your mind and good feelings in your heart. Keep love in your life, and you will find the love and light in everyone.

Be giving, forgiving, patient, and kind. Have faith in yourself. Be your own best friend, and listen to the voice that tells you to be your best self.

Be true to yourself in the paths that you choose. Follow your talents and passions; don't take the roads others say you must follow because they are the most popular. Take the paths where your talents will thrive — the ones that will keep your spirit alive with enthusiasm and everlasting joy.

Most of all, never forget that there is no brighter light than the one within you. Follow your inner light to your own personal greatness.

— Jacqueline Schiff

Find Happiness in Everything You Do

Find happiness in nature
in the beauty of a mountain
in the serenity of the sea
Find happiness in friendship
in the fun of doing things together
in the sharing and understanding
Find happiness in your family
in the stability of knowing
    that someone cares
in the strength of love and honesty
Find happiness in yourself
in your mind and body
in your values and achievements
Find happiness in
everything
you
do

— Susan Polis Schutz

Happiness cannot come from without. It must come from within. It is not what we see and touch or that which others do for us which makes us happy; it is that which we think and feel and do, first for the other fellow and then for ourselves.

— Helen Keller

Life is not measured by the number of breaths we take, but by the moments that take our breath away.

— Anonymous

Be Someone Who Changes the World

There are women who make things better... simply by showing up. There are women who make things happen. There are women who make their way. There are women who make a difference. And women who make us smile. There are women who do not make excuses. Women who cannot be replaced. There are women of wit and wisdom who — through strength and courage — make it through. There are women who change the world every day... women like you.

— Ashley Rice

Remember...
It's not how much you accomplish in life
that really counts,
but how much you give to others.
It's not how high you build your dreams
that makes a difference,
but how high your faith can climb.
It's not how many goals you reach,
but how many lives you touch.
It's not who you know that matters,
but who you are inside.

Live each day to its fullest potential,
and you can make a difference
in the world.

— Rebecca Barlow Jordan

Live Your World of Dreams

Lean against a tree
and dream your world of dreams
Work hard at what you like to do
and try to overcome all obstacles
Laugh at your mistakes
and praise yourself for learning from them

Pick some flowers
and appreciate the beauty of nature
Be honest with people
and enjoy the good in them
Don't be afraid to show your emotions
Laughing and crying make you feel better
Love your friends and family
    with your entire being
They are the most important part of your life
Feel the calmness on a quiet sunny day
and plan what you want to accomplish in life
Find a rainbow
and live your world of dreams

— Susan Polis Schutz

For My Grown-Up Daughter

It seems like yesterday
I tucked you in at night,
whispering a prayer of thanks
for another day of
having you in my life.

Not so long ago,
we were putting your baby teeth
out for the tooth fairy
and reading storybooks
until you fell asleep in my arms.
It felt as though
you grew overnight
into a beautiful young lady.

Today, Daughter,
I see you reaching out to people,
showing that one person
can make a difference in this world.
And what a difference you've made!
I know my life could never have been so
full and complete without your being
such an important part of it.
I've watched the difference you've made
in the lives of others as well.
You have a very special gift
that inspires people to be
the best they can be.
I'm so proud of all that you do,
and I hope you'll never forget that
I love you with all my heart!

— Carol Was

I Knew the Day Would Come

Of course I always knew
that someday you would be
a woman building your own life,
chasing dreams you've spent
    years creating.
You would sit across from me
and smile that smile
that would remind me of when
you were a little girl.

A million memories
would pass through my mind,
and I would be so proud
of who you've become
and so very thankful
to have been blessed to be
your parent.

And here we are.
It came just a little too fast —
I always knew it would.
But you are so beautiful,
and every time I look at you,
I am flooded with memories
    of your childhood
and awed by the woman
that you've become.

— Kellie L. McCracken

When a Daughter Becomes a Mother...

For so many years,
I couldn't even imagine
my daughter having a child!
It seemed as though
the best thing I could do for her
was to take care of her.
I know I fought her independence
    for a while,
because I enjoyed raising her so much.
I realize now, though,
that giving a daughter her independence
is the greatest show of love
    a mother can offer,
because it gives that daughter
the opportunity to realize
the joys of motherhood for herself.

My grandchildren are among my greatest joys,
and I am so proud of my daughter —
not only for having a child,
but for being a wonderful mother.
She has taught me that
the happiness she gives me now
is as great as the happiness she gave me
when she was a little girl —
it's just different...
in a very wonderful way.

— Vicki Perkins

Never Forget These Things, Daughter...

Your happiness, health, and safety
mean everything to me.

No matter how old you get,
I will always think of you as my child
and love you as much as ever.

I enjoy being with you
and am very pleased at the person
you've turned out to be.

You should always believe
that you are capable and worthy,
precious and unique —
and act accordingly.

You have touched my heart
and made me proud
more often than you could imagine.

Memories of you are very dear to me,
and sharing special times and traditions
makes them all the more enjoyable.

You bless my life in so many ways,
and I am thankful for the relationship
that we share.

There is nothing you could ever do
to lessen my love for you.

Being your parent has given me
happiness to the greatest degree
and warmth that fills my heart.
I am in awe that you came into my life
and made my dreams come true.

— Barbara Cage

You Have Blessed My Life Three Times Over

First... I love you as a daughter.

With all my heart, I know that no treasure will ever compare to the one I received... when you came into the world. You are a constant source of happiness and pride, and I will be grateful for everything about you each and every day of my life.

Second... I love you as a person.

With all the admiration I can possibly express, I want you to know what a truly remarkable person you are. I admire your dedication to all the right things, your devotion to your friends and family, the things you do, and the kindness that is such a sweet and natural part of you.

And third... I love you as a friend.

I can't tell you how happy it makes me to have a connection with you that is always there. It has a smiling, spontaneous, "just calling to say hi" aspect that the most heartwarming friendships all have. It has that kind of support and that kind of caring, and it's an uplifting and joyful connection I look forward to sharing with you forever.

— Laurel Atherton

Some Things About You Will Never Change

You may be grown now,
and you're a beautiful woman
in every way.
But occasionally I still see
the little girl in you
and realize that some things
never change.

It may be just the way
you turn your head
or a certain look in your eyes...

...but in that instant I'm reminded
that this woman is still my little girl.
In those moments,
a lifetime of love comes
sweeping through my heart —
and my feelings for you
grow deeper still.
We share a love that's certain
and a bond that will never break,
and I'm thankful that
those things will never change.
I know how blessed I am
to have you as a daughter.

— Cheryl Barker

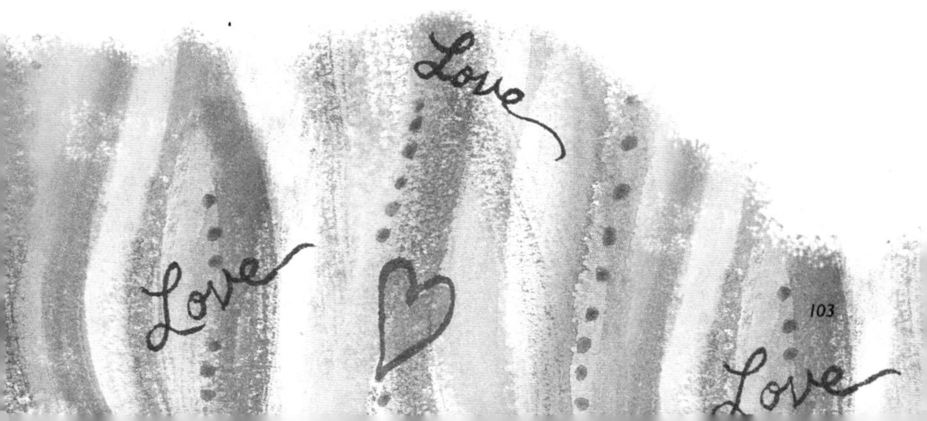

You Are Everything a Daughter Could Be

To have a daughter like you is to feel proud when I wake up each day. In spite of the mistakes I made in raising you, you never let them shape your future. You walked the path to success and triumphed with your positive attitude, your talents, and the lessons you learned.

To have a daughter like you is to feel peace in my heart. I don't have to hover over you, worry needlessly about you, or wonder if you're safe and secure. In the depths of my soul, I know you are a strong, capable, accomplished woman who is exactly where she wants to be in her life.

To have a daughter like you is to hear the music of joy and laughter wherever I go. Your can-do attitude, boundless energy, and enthusiasm for making the best of every situation are contagious and fun. Your spirited nature uplifts and inspires me.

To have a daughter like you is to be in the company of someone who holds my hand, gives me hugs, and walks with me through my troubles. In you, I have a special companion who shares with me an understanding of why we are blessed to have each other. To have a daughter like you is to walk with pride for all you are and with happiness in my heart for all we share.

— Jacqueline Schiff

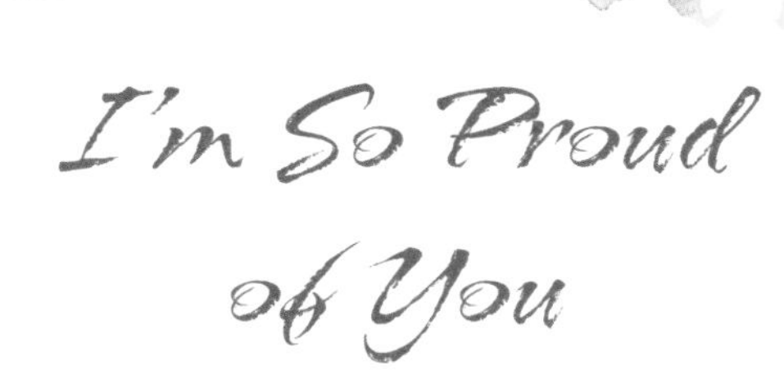

It seems that no matter what you undertake in life, you do so with a joyful and positive attitude. You work hard and try your best, pouring your heart into all you do. You demonstrate sincere gratitude and don't take your loved ones for granted. You never just "follow the crowd," and I admire the firm stand you take in maintaining your individuality.

— Debbie Burton-Peddle

Always know, Daughter... there is the gift of a hug waiting within my arms for you. I think sometimes even I forget that within the heart of the woman you've become, the child remains. And I want to hold you close and remind you of my love for you — which will forever remain in my heart.

— Teresa L. Davisson

Don't Ever Forget How Special You Are

Don't ever forget that you are unique.
Be your best self
and not an imitation of someone else.
Find your strengths
and use them in a positive way.
Don't listen to those
who ridicule the choices you make.
Travel the road that you have chosen
and don't look back with regret.
You have to take chances
to make your dreams happen.
Remember that there is plenty of time
to travel another road —
and still another —
in your journey through life.
Take the time to find the route
that is right for you.

You will learn something valuable
from every trip you take,
so don't be afraid to make mistakes.
Tell yourself that you're okay
just the way you are.
Make friends who respect your true self.
Take the time to be alone, too,
so you can know just how terrific
your own company can be.
Remember that being alone
doesn't always mean being lonely;
it can be a beautiful experience
of finding your creativity,
your heartfelt feelings,
and the calm and quiet peace
deep inside you.
And please don't ever forget
that you are special.

— Jacqueline Schiff

I Just Want You to Be Happy, Safe, and Secure

I want you to be well and at peace with yourself. I want you to get from life all that you desire and more. I want you to feel free to do whatever you want and to let that freedom soar. I want you to know love and be surrounded by it, to bear no pain and feel no hurt.

I want you to be the best person you can be. I want you to share the wonderful gift of yourself with others — how very lucky are those who will receive that beauty!

— Debbie Burton-Peddle

May You Be Blessed with All These Things...

A little more joy,
a little less stress,
a lot more recognition of
your wonderfulness.

Abundance in your life,
blessings in your days,
dreams that come true,
and hopes that stay.

A rainbow on the horizon,
an angel by your side...
and everything
that could ever bring
a smile to your life.

— Mia Evans

Carry These Special Feelings with You Always

Cheer to greet you each morning so each new day will help you believe that you are one step closer to your dreams.

Peace in your inner being so you can breathe easy and enjoy every moment of your life.

Faith to encourage and inspire you; to comfort you and heal your hurts; to commune with and be one with; to help you get in touch with your true self.

Laughter to bring you happiness and fun and keep your joy alive; to remind you that life is too short to spend it crying.

Beauty to fill your eyes with the simple gifts
that nature brings.

Confidence to do all the things that your true
self desires; to conquer your fears and be free
to reach your goals.

Friendships that are lasting and true with
people who respect your values and are full of
sharing and caring.

Memories of a life well lived that you can
reflect on and smile.

— Jacqueline Schiff

There Are Really No Words to Express the Love I Hold for You, Daughter

We have gone through many things together, you and I — some laced with pain and sadness, but most filled with the pure joy of our love for each other.

I remember how before you were born, I hoped for a daughter. Little did I know then that what I was really hoping for was a friend — someone to laugh with even when life was not funny, someone whose very presence would fill me with a love so deep and pure that I could finally understand what it meant to actually love someone more than I loved myself.

And now you are a young woman making a difference. Because of your presence, the world is simply a better place. Because of the love and care you show to others, lives are touched and changed. Because of the generosity of your spirit, others feel hope.

When I prayed for a daughter, I never imagined that I would get so much more.

— Lea Walsh

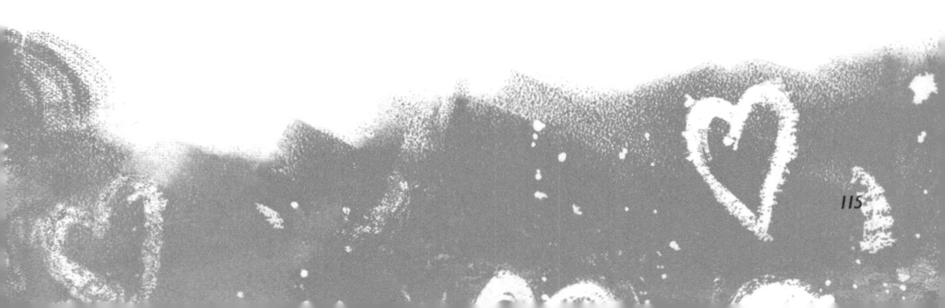

I Love You Every Minute of Every Day, My Beautiful Daughter

I looked at you today
and saw the same beautiful eyes
that looked at me with love
when you were a baby
I looked at you today
and saw the same beautiful mouth
that made me cry when you
first smiled at me
when you were a baby
It was not long ago
that I held you in my arms
long after you fell asleep
and I just kept rocking you
all night long

I looked at you today
and saw my beautiful daughter
no longer a baby
but a beautiful person
with a full range of emotions
feelings, ideas and goals
Every day is exciting
as I continue to watch you grow
I want you to always know that
in good and in bad times
I will love you
and that no matter what you do
or how you think
or what you say
you can depend on
my support, guidance
friendship and love
every minute of every day

— Susan Polis Schutz

Thanks for Giving Me This Chance to Let You Know...

You are a blessing I'm forever thankful for.
I love being with you,
and every time we're apart
there's a little part of me that stays with you.
Your sense of humor delights me.
Your laughter is one of my favorite sounds,
and your smiles light up my heart.
You go out of your way for others
and make a difference in the lives
of those you care about.
Being your parent
has been one of my greatest joys.

— Barbara Cage

Daughter,
I love you more than you know,
and I want everything beautiful
and wonderful for you.
I love being in your life and
sharing all that comes your way.
The love I have for you is so great
that I never have, and I never will,
take for granted the blessing
you have been to me.

I hope that as the years go by,
we will become even closer.
I couldn't have picked
a more precious daughter.
Thank you for giving me this chance
to say, "I love you,
and I will always be here for you."

— Mary Klock Labdon

You Are Such a Gift to My Life

You are generous, helpful, and kind.
Your sparkling personality
  lights up a room,
and when you are near,
  spirits are lifted.
It is said that we all need a little joy
every day of our lives.
Well, with the gift of you,
I have a lot of joy every single minute.

— Jacqueline Schiff

You are a shining
example of what a
daughter can be —
loving and compassionate
beautiful and good
honest and principled
determined and independent
sensitive and intelligent
You are a shining
example of what every
parent wishes their
daughter were
and I am so very
proud of
you

— Susan Polis Schutz

Daughter, You Are in My Heart Forever

The first time I held you in my arms and you wrapped your tiny hand around my index finger, I felt my heart swell with immeasurable joy and pride. I knew that my life had been touched in a miraculous way that would transform every dimension of it forever.

From the moment you were born, you became the focal point of my existence. Your smile was the sunshine in my heart. Your happiness was the only treasure I sought.

And so began the great paradox of parenthood. For when your tiny hand touched mine, I knew that I had been chosen to nurture you, love you, and then give you the strength to let go.

Letting go is not easy. But I look at you now — a beautiful young woman, strong in your convictions and determined to face life on your own terms — and I still feel my heart swell with pride and joy.

My dreams for your life might not always be the same ones you seek. But one thing remains the same: your happiness will always be my greatest treasure. I know now that the true miracle of that first touch lies in one simple truth: even though your hand may slip away from mine, we will hold each other in our hearts forever.

— Nancy Gilliam

ACKNOWLEDGMENTS

We gratefully acknowledge the permission granted by the following authors and authors' representatives to reprint poems or excerpts from their publications.

PrimaDonna Entertainment Corp. for "Don't Let Anything Steal Your Joy," "The heart needs friendship...," and "Ten Golden Rules to Help You Have a Better Life" by Donna Fargo. Copyright © 2005, 2006, 2008 by PrimaDonna Entertainment Corp. All rights reserved.

Rachel Snyder for "Remember Who You Are." Copyright © 2008 by Rachel Snyder. All rights reserved.

Jason Blume for "Keep Believing in Yourself, and Always Remember That I Believe in You, Too." Copyright © 2004 by Jason Blume. All rights reserved.

A careful effort has been made to trace the ownership of selections used in this anthology in order to obtain permission to reprint copyrighted material and give proper credit to the copyright owners. If any error or omission has occurred, it is completely inadvertent, and we would like to make corrections in future editions provided that written notification is made to the publisher:

BLUE MOUNTAIN ARTS, INC., P.O. Box 4549, Boulder, Colorado 80306.